STUDY GUIDE:
DITCH THE DRAMA

How to Access God's Promises of Joy and Freedom
No Matter What the World Throws at You

by

Ginny Priz

Study Guide: Ditch the Drama

ISBN-13: 978-0-692-29312-6
ISBN-10: 0-692-29312-4
www.ditchthedrama.net

Published with permission from WordCrafts Press (worcrafts.net) as ancillary material for Ditch the Drama: How To Access God's Promises of Joy and Freedom No Matter What The World Throws, Copyright © 2016

Contents

Acknowledgments

This study would not have been possible without Wordcrafts Press, who first published Ditch the Drama. I greatly appreciate their belief in me and the importance of these topics.

My heartfelt thanks to Paula Mosher Wallace whose walk with God inspires me daily. Her commitment to excellence has shaped the writing of this study and how I approach ministry.

For volunteering her time on this study guide and always encouraging me, I give a special thanks to Jean Przyborowski.

Introduction

Life is messy. Emotions are messy. Relationships are messy.

That's okay. They're supposed to be messy!

What they're not supposed to be is destructive. There's a fine line between the two, but if you know how to navigate the choppy waters internally and interpersonally, relationships can be a source of joy and freedom rather than drama.

Ditching life's drama is not about creating order around us or within us. It's about learning to navigate the messy emotions with God as our peaceful center.

Until I accepted messiness as a part of life, I spent all my time and energy trying to make my relationships fit into a nice, neat, controllable box! The process left me feeling trapped, confused, ashamed, and exhausted. Sound familiar?

Human relationships are as necessary to our healthy existence as food and water. And yet, most of us have not had any education on developing and maintaining healthy relationships. We generally adopt our good and bad emotional habits from watching our parents rather than learning from a collection of the best skills and habits in a classroom.

So, if you feel lost and confused about regulating your feelings and how to navigate relationships with difficult people, it's no wonder! Most adults are wandering around with only sufficient knowledge to get by.

Ditch the Drama and this study will revolutionize how you relate to God, yourself, and others around you. Your perspective and choices will change as you discover how to apply the truth inside the Serenity Prayer and develop the introspective and interpersonal skills you need to have incredibly healthy, fulfilling relationships.

Instead of feeling trapped and burdened, you will see how joy and freedom are the natural results of God's promises!

How It Works:
Each session you'll watch a short video, read the Session Notes and answer several discussion questions with your group. To access the videos, visit ditchthedrama.net or bloom-u.org.

Before the next session, answer the Homework Questions and read the next section of the *Ditch the Drama* book. Don't worry, the readings are short and to the point. It will only take you approximately twenty minutes each week.

The Serenity Prayer
by Reinhold Niebuhr

God,

Grant me the serenity to accept

the things I cannot change,

Courage to change the things I can,

and the Wisdom to know the difference,

Living one day at a time,

Enjoying one moment at a time,

Accepting hardship as a pathway to peace,

Taking, as Jesus did,

This sinful world as it is,

Not as I would have it,

Trusting that You will make all things right,

If I surrender to Your will,

So that I may be reasonably happy in this life,

And supremely happy with You forever in the next.

Amen.

Session 1:

Getting Started

SESSION NOTES:

I'm so glad you're here! Before we dive in, let's put first things first: close your eyes and take a deep breath!

Have you done it? Good. Now, take a few more deep breaths. You'll be glad you did.

When our attention is taken to the details and responsibilities of the day and pressure starts to build up in our emotions, our body will physically respond. There are a number of ways this shows up, but one of the most common is shallow breathing.

Taking a few deep breaths can help you slow down and refocus your mind. If you can, say a prayer at the same time. It will help keep you balanced physically and spiritually.

Creating a Safe Space

There is a room in my house I use as an office, but inevitably, because my work is ministry-focused, it becomes a prayer closet as well. I've made sure to have a comfortable desk, but also a comfortable couch where I work. The decorations are pieces that have special meaning to me and encourage me to follow God.

This is my safe space. What does your safe space look like? It doesn't have to be a room in your house. It can be a closet, bathroom, coffee shop, park bench, church building, car, corner in a library, or your kitchen table before your kids wake up. Your safe space could even be with a trusted friend or group of friends.

No matter where it is, your safe space should feel inviting to you and give you the opportunity to be you without being judged.

Over the next few weeks, we'll be addressing emotions and relationships that are likely to be frustrating or poke at some painful wounds. So it's important that you create a safe space to periodically retreat.

Creating a Safe Environment

If you are walking through this study with a small group, that's wonderful. It will give you the chance to see you are not alone in your struggles and walk the next few weeks of life together.

If you're joining me one-on-one for this journey, that's great too. You can go at your own pace and have a little more flexibility.

Either way, let's take this time to set expectations for this space and time together. While we are on this journey to ditch the drama, let's make this a safe environment. That means whether you're reading the materials, answering questions, or sitting in prayer, it will be a judgment-free, comparison-free, mask-free, shame-free environment!

Every time you feel judgment or comparison creeping in, toss them out! If shame or the desire to hide in fear comes calling, slam the door in their faces! You are God's beloved child and those around you are as well. So, in this space, let's treat each other like the beloved children we are

.

Create a Safe Mental Space

Safe environments are not just for your surroundings and small groups. They are for your mind as well.

We can often be our own worst critics. That internal criticism can prevent us from feeling safe enough to explore our own emotions. And that's not going to help anyone.

As you're working on ditching the drama, pay special attention to giving yourself grace rather than criticism. You'll find you'll move forward faster and be kinder to others as well.

Committing to the Process

Don't worry! You don't need to answer every question perfectly and no one will shame you for skipping homework assignments. Certainly, the questions will help you apply the material to your life, but this study is not about performance at all.

This commitment is to yourself, not to me or anyone else. It's a commitment to be kind and caring toward yourself while seeking the joy and freedom that is available.

Are you willing to:

- Take the time to truly look inward at yourself and your thoughts without judgment?
- Engage your heart and not just your mind?
- Intentionally be kind and encouraging to yourself?

You might not know exactly how to do all these things yet, and that's okay. If you decide to commit to this process, you're saying, "I will do my best to engage in these three areas, knowing it will not look perfect."

DISCUSSION QUESTIONS:

1. What do you hope to gain from going through this study?

2. How much time have you spent being introspective in the past? Will this be a new practice for you?

3. Do you have a safe space already? If not, what could you use as your safe space moving forward?

4. Share one positive statement about yourself.

PRAYER:

Heavenly Father,
I place my journey of ditching the drama at your feet. Thank you that I do not have to do everything perfectly and you will still love me and accept me. Help me to accept your grace as I look inward. Reveal to me what you would have me see and understand. I am willing to learn and grow in my relationships with you, myself, and others. In Jesus' name, Amen.

HOMEWORK QUESTIONS:

1. What emotions come up when you consider committing to looking inward, engaging your heart, and being kind to yourself during this journey?

2. Which commitment do you think will be the most difficult for you and why?

3. Which areas of your life are you fully trusting God to take care of?

4. In which areas of your life are you striving to figure it all out, make it happen, look better, or feel better about?

READING FOR NEXT SESSION IN *DITCH THE DRAMA*:

- Preface
- Introduction

I am grateful for:

Wisdom I've learned:

What I am surrendering to God:

What I can actually change:

Scripture verse I will focus on to help me trust God:

Action steps I will take to improve my relationship with myself and God:

Action steps I will take to improve my relationship with others:

Session 2:

Deconstructing Drama

SESSION NOTES:

Drama:
Any unnecessary conflict, whether it be internal or interpersonal.

Yes, that's right, not all conflict is bad. Conflict can be necessary to reach a more peaceful end.

I can just imagine some of you cringing and shifting in your seats as you read that. Conflict may have actually been your entire definition of drama. Sorry to disappoint you, but it's a little more complicated than that.

To conflict (the verb) means there are two things that differ or clash or are incompatible. A conflict (the noun) describes a fight between two sides of an issue. The two concepts are separate. Just because two things do not agree, does not mean they are in a battle.

Which "conflict" am I describing in the definition of drama above? Both. Both unnecessary disagreements and unnecessary fighting are drama.

The nuances of each definition will be addressed throughout the study. For now, let's focus on our relationship with God and on how identifying disagreements can help us ditch the drama.

Now, Adam and Eve had a nice set up! They were living in a beautiful, lush garden in perfect relationship with God. They were completely in His will until the serpent lied to them and gave them some false ideas about what God meant.

The next thing you know, they've eaten from the forbidden tree. This immediately brought in shame, fear and guilt. That's when drama officially entered the world!

Why? Because that is the moment when humans decided to walk outside of God's will.

Why isn't the serpent's temptation the first instance of drama? Because if Adam and Eve had decided to stick with God's plan and stay inside His will, it would have necessitated a disagreement between them and Satan. And that conflict would have born great fruit.

Instead, Adam and Eve were deceived rather than standing their ground in a conflict. God and sin will always conflict. There can be no sin in Him; it is impossible.

Before or after the fall, staying in God's will is still the safest place for us to be. God is our protector and provider. Therefore, if we want to remain in His best plan for our lives, we will have to choose conflict with temptation and sin in the world around us.

> *"Trust in the Lord with all your heart and lean not on your own understanding; in all your ways submit to him, and he will make your paths straight."*
>
> Psalm 3:5-6

Moving in the ways of the world rather than in God's will creates a ripple effect that is essentially drama. This goes for every human on the planet. And that's a lot of ripples (right?), because no one is perfect.

On the other hand (no pun intended), God can use us to dampen or stop ripples completely by surrendering to His will and walking in step with Him. There is hope!

We are not useless or powerless against these ripples. God and the Holy Spirit can work through you to render some of that drama powerless.

Every time you stepped out in faith, you were fighting drama. Every time you forgave your enemies or debtors, you won a victory over drama. Every time you lived according to God's promises, drama didn't even have a chance to start.

Trusting the Lord and living according to His word may not be popular. Your choices may be in conflict with the opinions of people around you. Don't be tempted to react to the drama they create. It's not your responsibility to make sure they agree with you or do the "right" thing.

DISCUSSION QUESTIONS:

1. How do you feel about conflict in general? Would you be more comfortable creating conflict with people rather than living in conflict with God?

2. How often do you feel like you are responsible for the results of a situation (making something happen) rather than just being responsible for the piece God asked you to contribute (love others, step out in faith, etc.)?

3. Have you ever considered how your thoughts influence your emotions and actions? What kind of decisions have you made when your thoughts were focused on trusting God?

PRAYER:

Heavenly Father,
Please forgive me for the ways I have stepped outside of your will, knowingly or unknowingly. This world is so broken and it can be discouraging to look at the ripple effects of sin. But I will not let discouragement take root in my heart. You are on the throne and working in all things for my good! Thank you for giving me the free will to choose love instead of lies! Thank you for the opportunity to fight sin and drama in this world through surrender! I place all the outcomes at the foot of the cross of Your Son, Jesus Christ, and I trust You to lead the way!
In Jesus' name, Amen.

HOMEWORK QUESTIONS:

1. One way to describe drama would be as "the echoes of sin." Where have you seen the ripple effect of others' sins impact your life?

2. Where have you seen the ripple effect of your personal sin impact the lives of those around you?

3. How would your life look different if you lived as if God's promises were true? What kind of daily decisions would you change?

4. In what areas of your journey with God have you refused His guidance or refused to follow Jesus' teaching (been disobedient)?

5. Describe a time when you trusted God and felt His peace.

READING FOR NEXT SESSION IN DITCH THE DRAMA:

- Chapter 1 (God)
- Chapter 2 (Grant Me)
- Chapter 3 (The Serenity)

I am grateful for:

Wisdom I've learned:

What I am surrendering to God:

What I can actually change:

Scripture verse I will focus on to help me trust God:

Action steps I will take to improve my relationship with myself and God:

Action steps I will take to improve my relationship with others:

Session 3:

God, Grant Me the Serenity

EXERCISE REVIEW:

- Share about your experience with the Empathy Exercise in *Ditch the Drama*. **What did you learn about yourself?**

SESSION NOTES:

God

God blows my mind. He is all powerful and all love. He is everywhere and inside us. He knows all our sins and still offers unending grace. He imagined each of us before we were born. He loved and valued us with such intensity that He chose to bring us into existence so He could spend eternity in heaven with us.

I say "us" because I know God feels this way about all His children. But have you ever stopped to claim this for yourself? Make it personal. God does.

How generous He is to want a personal relationship! He used dozens of authors over thousands of years to write you (yes you) His love letter – the Bible. He sent His son, Jesus, who was fully God and man to teach us about His love. He actually spoke the words that taught us how we can receive joy and freedom.

He was willing to die on the cross and fully separate from God the Father to take on your sin. Why? Because He couldn't stand the idea of being without you in heaven.

Whenever I sit and take the time to reflect on God and His love story, my perspective shifts off my weakness and onto His magnificent strength. The problems that seem to engulf my life come into perspective as minute details for God to work out.

For me, this time of reflection comes most easily when I look at the sky. The magnitude of its expanse reminds me of all He is capable of making and orchestrating. I can rest knowing that God is willing and able to take care of me and my worries. He

doesn't expect me to have the solutions and perform perfectly along the way. Relief and hope wash over me because He is:

- Consistently patient
- Constantly loving
- Completely passionate about my personal journey

Grant Me

It is only by God's amazing grace that we can ask Him for anything.

God was very intentional about all of His creation. He didn't just slap it all together haphazardly. He took the time to assemble the elements and cells and atoms. Everything on earth has a system with boundaries, as does the kingdom of heaven.

God the Father has been teaching us about the kingdom of heaven through the Bible, Jesus, and the Holy Spirit for over six thousand years. That tells me He's invested in helping us understand how this all works together.

God is perfect and without sin. He cannot exist in the same space as sin. Therefore, when we sin, we are pulling ourselves further and further away from God. This is so harmful to us and so important for us to understand that God put drastic measures in place. He required a death to reconcile us to Him.

Instead of requiring the sinner to die, He was gracious to the Israelites by providing stand-ins through sacrifices on an altar. Eventually, in His perfect timing, God sent His son to be the ultimate stand-in for the deaths required for all our sins.

All of the sacrifices God asked for were not about making Him happy. They were for our education about the kingdom of heaven. They were to demonstrate how harmful and devastating the effects of sin could be since we could not see this clearly with our eyes.

According to our actions, what each of us deserves is death. Our sins are not washed away by simple repentance, but by a God who moved heaven and earth to make repentance possible. The fact that He allows us to ask anything of Him is a miracle. That God desires us to pray without ceasing is proof of His divine love.

God has done all of this to guide you toward a closer relationship with Him where you'll be safe in His will. So, when you authentically pray for guidance to stay in His will, you are aligning with God and He will answer those prayers.

Instead of continuously praying for what you want (which is usually the fastest way to comfort, power, or approval), what if you prayed for the wisdom and strength to walk in His will? You may not like how God guides or answers your prayer. He may ask you to step outside your comfort zone or take you in a completely new direction. But I can promise you it will be worth it.

In the years that I have embraced this kind of surrendered prayer, my life has turned upside down. God opened the door for me to anchor *Bloom Today*, an international television show. This was way outside my comfort zone! Now, He has me as a host on THREE television shows. At the same time, He asked me to deplete my savings account and start living by faith. It's really been a rollercoaster!

At the same time, I have experienced miracles, been healed from old trauma, and received more hope, joy, and freedom than I ever could have dreamed were possible.

We may not find God's methods comfortable, but we cannot argue with the results!

The Serenity

I cannot tell you how many different ways I tried to achieve serenity before I found surrender. I strove and performed and tried to earn serenity as best I could. I wasted countless hours and tons of money hoping the next thing would work.

Finally, God explained to me that serenity isn't something that's earned. Rather, it's the natural result of a choice to surrender to Him.

My reaction was to cringe. That felt wrong. How could I gain something by inviting chaos into my life? Because surely chaos would result if I wasn't on my game and creating the "right" conditions or performing in just the "right" way. I argued that I would slip into despair or become mean and heartless unless I was controlling myself 24/7.

Obviously, God won that argument. I stopped striving for my will. I stopped trying to control what other people said, did or thought about me. I stopped trying to force the outcomes I wanted. I stopped trying to change the past or create a specific future.

I slowed down. I did a lot of waiting. I prayed a lot. I listened to the Holy Spirit a lot. I practiced trusting God's plan. I paid more attention to the present moment. I stopped taking care of adults who weren't asking for my help. And whenever I caught myself trying to take control again, I stopped – again and again and again.

And once I got through the initial discomfort of feeling out of control, I realized the world didn't fall apart. Life was still okay if circumstances didn't go my way. I wasn't heartless. I didn't fall into apathy. Others survived and learned lessons just fine without me. Bonus points: there was no angry mob demanding that I go back to forcing my will (which, oddly enough, I kind of expected).

The relief that comes with full surrender is incredible! So, why aren't more people doing this? Because surrender also clears the way for emotions to come to the surface. All that running around and striving is a big distraction from feeling and processing the impact of what we've experienced.

Clearing the way for emotions may not feel great at first. Some of you have been running from emotions for a long time, like I did. In that case, there will be more to feel and process.

But this also opens the door to all of the positive emotions: joy, hope, gratitude, glee, contentment, peace, and love!

It's important to remember that emotions are not part of our identity. They are tools given to us by God to help us understand what we experience.

I'll talk more about how to navigate painful emotions in the next session. Until then, keep giving them to God!

DISCUSSION QUESTIONS:

1. How much time do you spend reflecting on God's love and sovereignty on an average weekday? How could your outlook improve if you increased that time?

2. What is preventing you from fully embracing the Father's love completely?

3. Do you spend more of your mental bandwidth trying to figure out the past or the future?

4. Read Romans 15:13. In this passage Paul tells us when we trust in God the Holy Spirit can fill us with hope, joy, and peace. God does not ask us to manufacture these feelings on our own, but rather receive from Him by trusting in Him. Have you ever tried to manufacture these feelings yourself? How?

PRAYER:

Heavenly Father,
You know the desires of my heart even better than I do myself. I realize these desires may not be in line with your best will for my life. Please remove from me any longings that are not aligned with Your plan. Thank you for the blessings You have already provided and the blessings I have not yet seen. I trust your plan is better than mine, and I surrender to it.
In Jesus' name, Amen.

HOMEWORK QUESTIONS:

1. How do feel about surrendering your will for God's best?

2. What is preventing you from fully embracing how wide and deep is the Father's love?

3. Have you been asking God to bless your ideas of how your life "should" look? Explain.

4. How would your life look different if you let God pour hope, joy, and peace into you each morning?

5. Is it difficult for you to wait and listen for God to reveal His will to you? Why or why not?

6. What do you think you could gain from spending more time focusing on the present?

7. God's plan is better than our own. Can you see any ways that God might be using pain to be part of a healing process or transition? Like pain after surgery?

8. Where have you been feeling sorry for yourself? Ask God to come into those hurting places and help you see past your emotions.

READING FOR NEXT SESSION IN DITCH THE DRAMA:

- Chapter 4 (To Accept)

I am grateful for:

Wisdom I've learned:

What I am surrendering to God:

What I can actually change:

Scripture verse I will focus on to help me trust God:

Action steps I will take to improve my relationship with myself and God:

Action steps I will take to improve my relationship with others:

Session 4:

To Accept

EXERCISE REVIEW:

- Share about your experience with the Feel Your Emotions Exercise in *Ditch the Drama*. ***What did you learn about yourself and your emotions?***

SESSION NOTES:

Until I learned how to navigate my emotions in healthy ways, they felt like the black, jumbled mess on the cover of this book. They were confusing, overwhelming, and scary. I was sure they would only grow in strength and number if I looked at them, so I resolved to ignore them instead. I had no idea I was only creating more drama.

Everything Is Connected

Your core beliefs are connected to your thoughts, and your thoughts are connected to your feelings. All three affect your behaviors.

If you refuse to examine your emotions, thoughts, and beliefs, then you'll never understand your behaviors. You also won't gain the ability to improve those behaviors.

Take the journey to renew your mind. Accept what is under the surface so that you can leverage those thoughts and emotions. This way, you can experience a life of freedom.

Emotions:

- Emotions may feel overwhelming sometimes, but you are not their victim. With practice, you can use them to help you gain peace.
- Emotions are warning signs indicating how your thoughts and beliefs are lining up with God's truth.
- Emotions are not a judgment of your character or value.
- Feeling your emotions and paying attention to them will help you identify your thoughts. Then you'll be able to discern whether your beliefs are aligning with truth or lies.

- When your beliefs are not aligned with truth, there is disruption in your mind, body, and spirit. Until you have resolved the issue, the disruption will take up precious bandwidth. This will affect your ability to be peacefully present and process new information and feelings. Like a clog in a pipe, it affects the whole system.
- Your thoughts and emotions are reflected in your body. Your body being tense, ill, or in pain can likely be traced back to an emotion and belief that is not in alignment with Biblical truth.
- The thoughts behind your emotions may seem very real even though they do not align with scripture. Remember, you are not a victim at the mercy of your thoughts. With repetition, you can choose to believe and embrace the truth found in scripture.
- Learning to discover what each emotion feels like and how best to handle it is a process. Give yourself grace as you discover and explore unfamiliar thoughts and emotions.
- Emotions don't go away when we ignore them. Trying to stuff them or shut them down will only delay feeling them.
- Grief is a messy and unpredictable process. How you travel through the process does not determine your value, performance, or abilities.
- The emotions you feel as you grieve are still a reflection of your thoughts and beliefs. Taking those thoughts captive and making them obedient to Christ will help you navigate the process faster.
- Negative emotions that seem to attack your identity are not from God and not a part of grieving. The thoughts connected to them sound like "I suck." "I'm stupid." "I'm not good enough." They are straight lies about yourself even when the feel real. No matter your past, God loves you, and the truth is that you are valuable. These emotions are not healthy to wallow in or explore. Replace them with scriptural truth immediately every time.

Grief

The brokenness of this world is often difficult to accept. And in those seasons of struggling to understand why God allows the pain, our anger and frustration rise. This is part of the grieving process. The important thing to remember is to keep taking that anger and frustration to God.

I've undergone many seasons where I blame God for pain that accompanies "the things I cannot change." I've felt alone and rejected because God has yet to provide a

husband. I've been nearly suffocated by narcissistic and codependent friends. I've even burned out from the pressures of ministry.

As I bring each frustration and sadness to God, He doesn't fight back or accuse. He is quiet and patient. And when I have exhausted my complaints and grown tired of the pity party, God reminds me of His love and His character. My heart is inevitably softened and convicted by His consistent nature.

I recognize, once again, that God is in charge. He knows much more than I do, after all. He sees all things, knows all things, and has my ultimate best in mind. I wonder why I've been clinging so desperately to my own will. I finally accept His instead.

There is peace in acceptance. Even though, at first, it can sting slightly to accept His will, there is a deep, abiding peace that is unmistakable. That peace brings healing to our hearts in this new chapter of acceptance.

DISCUSSION QUESTIONS:

1. What has this lesson helped you discover about emotions?

2. Discuss how emotions, even painful ones, can be great blessings.

3. What has been your experience with grief in the past?

4. Have you ever intentionally grieved anything besides a person or pet that passed?

PRAYER:

Heavenly Father,
Thank you for creating emotions as a way for me to understand your heart and come into closer relationship with you. I don't always know how to deal with my emotions in the best way, so I ask you to give me insight. Please help me to be aware of my feelings without shame or judgment. Show me where they are aligned with You and where they are not. Give me wisdom to discern how best to navigate them.
In Jesus' name, Amen.

HOMEWORK QUESTIONS:

1. Have you judged yourself by your thoughts or emotions in the past? When?

2. You are God's precious child; that cannot change. Your thought patterns and feelings can change as you grow. How does this truth make you feel?

3. Describe your relationship with your emotions. Do you embrace any of them? Fear any of them? Avoid any of them? Ignore any of them? Stuff any of them?

4. What role have your emotions played in your decision-making in the past?

5. What can you do to make sure your emotions are playing a helpful role in your life rather than a destructive one?

READING FOR NEXT SESSION IN *DITCH THE DRAMA*:

- Chapter 5: The Things I Cannot Change
- Chapter 6: The Courage

I am grateful for:	Wisdom I've learned:
What I am surrendering to God:	What I can actually change:

Scripture verse I will focus on to help me trust God:

Action steps I will take to improve my relationship with myself and God:	Action steps I will take to improve my relationship with others:

Session 5:

The Things I Cannot Change, The Courage

EXERCISE REVIEW:

- Share about your experience with the Affirming God's Promises Exercise in *Ditch the Drama*. **What did you discover about God?**
- Share about your experience with the What God Says About You Exercise in *Ditch the Drama*. **Which statements resonated with you and which did not?**

SESSION NOTES:

When I began studying the Serenity Prayer in the early days of my recovery, I didn't give too much thought to the "things I couldn't change." It seemed obvious that there would be things I couldn't change.

When I was asked to list everything I was *trying* to change, I expected a nice, short list. What I got was a wakeup call.
I realized below the surface all my decisions were motivated by a desire to control the world around me. I was shocked.

At first, I tried to downplay my need to control. After all, mine was rarely a take-charge, dominating approach. I opted, instead, for passive attempts to get what I wanted. Yet, the longer I looked at the list, the more I realized this constant hoping and trying for change was creating my inner turmoil.

To control my financial security, I was working long hours and literally making myself sick. To control my social status, I was a supportive, even enabling, friend. To control the number of blessings I received from God, I went to church and stuffed all my anger. To control my "inner peace," I drank to numb out. Clearly, I was operating in insanity.

Consciously or not, I believed the only way to feel good enough was to create security in and around me. And when you're judging your value and success by the way the

world responds, it's no wonder you feel desperate to control the world. This kind of thinking creates desperation to change that which we are powerless over.

Thankfully, the Serenity Prayer reminded me I could live another way. I could surrender worldly security and my emotions to God's will. I could trust Him and embrace the value He places on me instead.

The Things I Cannot Change
We could spend eternity listing all the "things we cannot change." But of all those items, the one I'm most grateful to have on the list is God.

> *"The Lord is my rock, my fortress and my deliverer;*
> *my God is my rock, in whom I take refuge,*
> *my shield and the horn of my salvation, my stronghold."*
>
> Psalm 18:2

Life's challenges and struggles will take our focus away from God and His promises. That is the nature of living in a broken world. But whenever we are willing to turn back to God, He is always willing to welcome us into closer relationship. Thank goodness nothing we can say or do will persuade Him to turn His back on us.

We humans are constantly changing our minds, acting out of self-interest, and creating drama. Being surrounded by that brokenness, it can be difficult to trust God's nature. Despite our doubts, God stays fixed. He chooses to love us rather than control us.

I cannot imagine God choosing love over control despite watching us make painful mistakes. There's a fine line between love and control. How many times have you been so frustrated with someone's choices that you intervened? How many times have you criticized to prove your point? Repeatedly "suggested" a solution until you won?

Even if our goal is to help the other person, we can still slip into control if we aren't careful.

Are you trying to make a disciple? Then love them until they want to hear about Jesus. Are you wanting to restore a sinner gently? Then speak out of love, and leave the rest to God. Are you training up a child in the way they should go? Then love them where they are and encourage them in the right direction.

It's easy to see why we drift toward the responsibility of changing others. But, in the end, we are called to love and not to control.

A personal connection with God through the Holy Spirit is ultimately what brings change. So relax. The pressure is off. God is using many strategies to touch the hearts of His children and convict them. He wants you to participate in the story, but He doesn't need you to accomplish His plan. The universe is not resting on your shoulders.

When our motivation is to love and accept, the atmosphere changes. The people around us feel at ease and open to learning, rather than guarded and defensive. The key is to stay aware of your motivation. If you're using "love" to get what you want, you're walking in a spirit of control.

Love isn't a tool to be used like a crowbar to get others to do what I want. Love is a gift that fills others with the joy and freedom we've already received. Through this pouring out, others will have the choice to accept God's love or reject it. They have the choice to be convicted or not.

Either way, the results are not our responsibility. Our responsibility is to love and point toward God. We can only let go and accept what others choose.

Courage
Courage is relative. One person's greatest fear is another's leisurely afternoon.

If you are judging your personal courage by someone else's gauge, then you'll never measure up. Keep your eyes on your own journey. Reflect on where you've made the hard choice to keep your integrity. Ask God to remind you of all the steps you've taken while still scared. I'd be willing to bet there are a lot more courageous decisions in your story than you give yourself credit for.

Remember, God has not given you a spirit of fear. He doesn't want you to be overwhelmed or stuck because of fear. In God's design, fear was created to be a momentary survival mechanism. It was never meant to rule our lives and decisions.

So why is it so many of us think worry is a necessary part of love? Why do we wear stress as a badge of importance?

I understand if you are anxious or stressed on a regular basis; it is not a choice you can just stop cold turkey. Your brain and emotions have created a whole lot of ruts in the fear department. Trying to stop them would be like trying to stop a freight train with your face: neither pleasant nor effective.

Instead, each time you feel the fear train coming, redirect your focus toward God. He is your mighty protector and provider. He is big enough to redirect the train. Doesn't that sound much more pleasant and effective?

Since Jesus is the author and perfecter of our faith, we can stop trying to conjure courage from thin air. We can, however, start receiving it by choosing to surrender to God and embrace His promises.

At some point, God *will* ask you to step outside your comfort zone. When He does, keep your eyes on God and expect Him to meet you there. Each step you take will reinforce your faith and your courage. Celebrate every baby step.

DISCUSSION QUESTIONS:

1. What have you tried to change that was out of your control?

2. How have you loved with the singular motivation to give instead of control?

3. How did you feel after taking each of those actions? What was different?

4. Share one or two courageous actions you've taken recently.

PRAYER:

Heavenly Father,
I come to you with all my cares and burdens. I am striving to change so many things outside of my control. As I surrender them and leave them in your capable hands, help me to trust you to protect and provide. I believe you are trustworthy. I believe you are bigger than my fears and will meet me at every step you ask me to take. Thank you for going ahead of me to make a way.
In Jesus' name, Amen.

HOMEWORK QUESTIONS:

1. Who have you been trying to change, directly or indirectly?

2. What "successful" outcomes have you been trying to make happen?

3. Reflect on God's immense love and His complete, eternal, and uncompromising promises. How can you start to intentionally remind yourself of these daily?

4. How is God asking you to have the courage to trust Him and step outside your comfort zone in this season of your life?

5. When you take a step of faith in obedience, it is God's responsibility to take care of the consequences and results. How does that knowledge change your perspective on what God is asking you to do?

6. What courageous decision will you make to step into God's will this week?

READING FOR NEXT SESSION IN *DITCH THE DRAMA*:

- Chapter 7: To Change the Things I Can (Part 1)
  - ○ Stop reading after the Reaction Awareness Exercise.

I am grateful for:

Wisdom I've learned:

What I am surrendering to God:

What I can actually change:

Scripture verse I will focus on to help me trust God:

Action steps I will take to improve my relationship with myself and God:

Action steps I will take to improve my relationship with others:

Session 6:

To Change

EXERCISE REVIEW:

- Share about your experience with the Reaction Awareness Exercise in *Ditch the Drama*. **What did you discover about yourself?**

SESSION NOTES:

> *"Search me, God, and know my heart;*
> *test me and know my anxious thoughts.*
> *See if there is any offensive way in me,*
> *and lead me in the way everlasting."*

Psalm 139:23-24

Are you willing to examine your thoughts and emotions? Are you willing to see where your perspectives and reactions have led you away from God?

For a long time, I was terrified to look at my flaws for what they were. I thought I would have to carry the shame and guilt of them all the days of my life. Owning them felt like an impossible burden that would never cease. But I was wrong.

God asks us to identify our shortcomings so we can heal and be free from the shame and guilt. We can fully accept His forgiveness. We do not have to stay stuck in our old ways of thinking or behaving.

What Is Your Perspective of Yourself?

None of us will ever be perfect, and none of us will ever be worthless. Let's throw out those two extremes right now. Stop judging yourself between them. It's an illusion that will have you trapped in a performance mindset.

Instead, we're all on a journey somewhere between where we were and where God

is taking us. He's not surprised by where we are. He has actually tailored His plan accordingly.

> *"Do not conform to the pattern of this world, but be transformed by the renewing of your mind. Then you will be able to test and approve what God's will is—his good, pleasing and perfect will."*

Romans 12:12

There are so many messages coming from the world that we can begin to believe them if we're not careful. For example, we may believe we are unworthy of a raise because our boss refuses to give one. We might doubt our ability to be a good friend if one of them is mad at us. Or, we may begin to feel unlovable after a divorce.

As children of God, we must renew our minds with scripture. The living word can free us from the ever-changing opinions of the world. By continuously comparing our perspectives to Biblical truth, we can discern truth from drama.

By keeping the truth close, we will begin to see ourselves as God sees us. He sees us fully forgiven on a journey of transformation.

What Is Your Perspective of Others?

It is so easy to put labels on those around us. We do this to make sense of ourselves, our relationships, and our place in the world. Labels can help us navigate social interactions and help us reach our goals. But they are not always a help.

Simplistic and rigid labels will keep us from loving our neighbors. We could potentially begin to condemn or elevate others due to false assumptions. That's dangerous because the temptation to take advantage of others is stronger if we've reduced them to labels.

When all the labels are stripped away, the truth is simple. God is on the throne. The rest of us are broken humans on the same playing field. We may look and act differently, but we were all created as children of God. All of us are looking for love and acceptance.

The more we see each other without the labels, the more we can respect each other. Ultimately, this means the more drama we can ditch.

The Karpman Drama Triangle
Reflect on the Victim, Rescuer, and Aggressor roles found in the Karpman Drama Triangle.

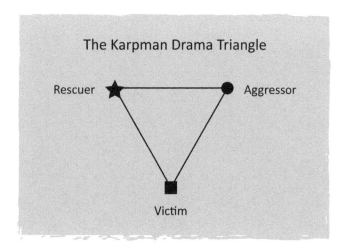

Perspective plays a leading role in all our lives. How we see ourselves and others determines how we behave in relationships. If we are all God's children on equal footing, then there is never a need to see ourselves as above or below another human being. But this is still a broken world. And influences to the contrary appear every day.

If you see yourself as a victim, then you'll likely feel hopeless and powerless. Those feelings will keep you stuck in silence. They will steal your voice and your motivation to change.

Even if you do not normally see yourself in these roles, stay vigilant. It doesn't take much to be drawn in to this power struggle with the right person.

While this triangle demonstrates a power struggle amongst a group of three, life is not always as straight forward as a perfect triangle.

No one is ever locked into one role in the triangle across all relationships. A person might see themselves as the victim in their marriage and become an aggressor with their children.

Rescuers can perceive themselves as being in all three roles over the course of the struggle:

1) Rescuer to the Victim
2) Aggressor to the Aggressor
3) Victim of the Aggressor

Take a look at the Flip-Flopping Roles illustration. Even when there are only two parties, the principle still applies. Each person takes turns being rescuer and victim.

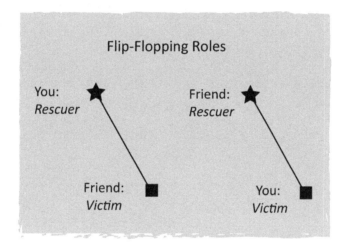

This scenario is unhealthy because neither person is empowering the other to come out of their rescuer or victim mentalities. The rescuer gets their fix from feeling needed. The victim gets their fix from pity.

The cycle continues because personal responsibility for shortcomings is not taken. Real change or action is never encouraged.

Next, consider the Alternating Roles Illustration. The location of the victim role is very specific because everyone in the triangle sees the victim as lower.

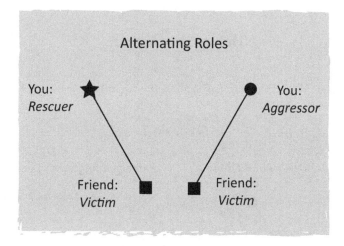

If the victim shows no signs of improvement or appreciation, the rescuer will eventually be sucked dry of every bit of patience. Without healthy boundaries in place, the rescuer will eventually lose their ever-lovin' mind and unleash their inner aggressor. And the echoes of drama continue.

Finally, take a look at the illustration titled Below the Surface on the following page. These scenarios show how each person in the situation can perceive everyone's roles differently.

In scenario 1 on the left-hand side, we see the victim is accusing the aggressor and appealing to the rescuer for help. From the outside, this scenario seems fairly straightforward. But what if the "aggressor" is innocent of the accusation?

On the righthand side, we see how the roles change from the "aggressor's" point of view. In the "aggressor's" mind, they are the victim and the "victim" calling for help is seen as the aggressor.

Everyone in the triangle will have their own perspective. Everyone in the triangle will think they are right. That's why it's so important to see yourself and others outside the triangle entirely.

No matter who is perceived to have all the power, the truth is God has all of it. Surrender to His plan. Resist the temptation to get sucked in to the drama.

Below the Surface

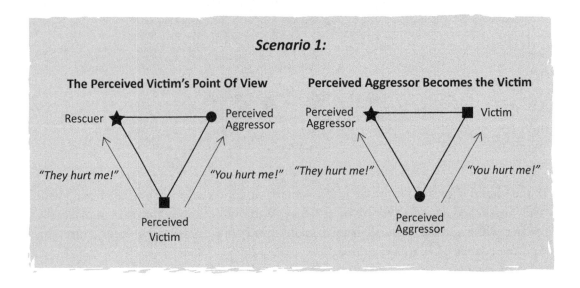

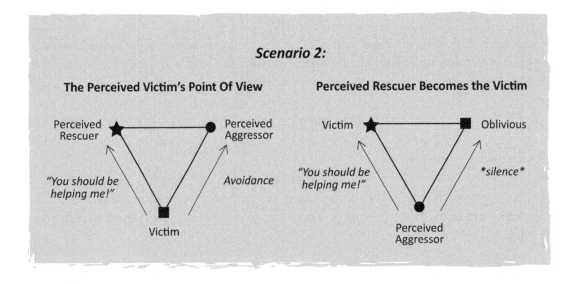

Scenario 2 demonstrates how a rescuer can begin to see themselves as a victim. They feel stuck in the rescuer role. This happens when the rescuer is unable to draw healthy boundaries as the victim sucks the life out of them.

This power dynamic is easy to fall into as soon as one person in any relationship believes these labels are reality. When someone begs for your help and puts you on a pedestal, the temptation is to help that person. A rescuer is born! And when someone accuses you of harmful behavior, it's hard not to lash out. The aggressor appears!

The good news is that these roles are not permanent! We can work to change our personal perspectives. We can use our voice to communicate in love and stay out of the triangle.

Remember, healthy individuals are approachable and are able to calmly discuss relationship dynamics. Unhealthy individuals often refuse to see any perspective outside their own. Instead, they'll stay in denial, accuse to deflect blame, or simply react aggressively.

If anyone behaves in an unhealthy manner consistently, then for your own sanity keep them at arm's-length (or two arm's-lengths if possible). If you cannot cut ties entirely, then just expect to have unhealthy reactions from them. Ask God to help you see them in love and treat them with respect, despite their choices. Ask Him as many times as you need. He will not grow tired of you.

If you've fallen into triangle trap, you can start to get free by taking the following steps:
- Address others with love
- Respect all others despite their behaviors
- Stop making assumptions about what others think or feel
- Victims: Remember you always have a choice. Believing you are powerless will only continue the cycle and keep you stuck.
- Aggressors: Rather than trying to force others to conform to your way of thinking, trust that God will keep you safe without control. No matter what others choose to do or say, God deems you valuable. And that's sufficient.
- Rescuers: Trust that God will encourage and equip others to overcome their challenges – even if it means the situation will get worse before it gets better. Your helping or commiserating may be getting in the way of what God is doing. Instead, keep pointing others to God.

If we are relying on our reactions rather than considered responses, the Karpman Drama Triangle is the inevitable trap we fall into. But, it's not impossible to remain drama-free!

Stand on your identity in Christ. Accept the things and people you cannot change. Act with a considered response. Over time, you may be surprised at how much drama is curbed by practicing these behaviors. It may be difficult at first. But your muscles will soon build, and you'll be deflecting more drama than you ever thought possible.

DISCUSSION QUESTIONS:

1. Share how the Karpman Drama Triangle or any of the illustrated variations have shown up in your life.

2. On your own sheet of paper, write a list of the shortcomings you want to change.

3. On a second sheet of paper, write what you will do instead.

4. Tear up the first piece of paper with your shortcomings on it and throw the pieces in the trash.

5. Share what you wrote on the second piece of paper with your group or a trusted friend.

PRAYER:

Heavenly Father,
I repent for seeing others as above me or below me. I want to see myself and others as You see us. Show me how to do this so I may love your children rather than get caught in a power struggle. I trust Your Holy Spirit to help me break free of the temptation as it arises. Guide my words and actions to be more like Jesus.
In Jesus' name, Amen.

HOMEWORK QUESTIONS:

1. What are some of the emotions and thoughts you've begun to reflect on regularly as a result of this study?

2. What are some of the thoughts you've recognized that do NOT line up with God's promises?

3. For each thought that does not line up with God's heart, write down a scripture that reveals the truth.

4. Have you ever been involved in the kind of relationship illustrated in the Karpman Drama Triangle? Which role(s) have you played and with whom?

5. Think about the people in your life that you are most comfortable and uncomfortable with. Have you assigned them a label in your mind? How has this label affected how you see them or treat them?

6. Can you look beyond the label to see them as a child of God separate from their choices?

READING FOR NEXT SESSION IN *DITCH THE DRAMA*:

- Chapter 7: To Change the Things I Can
    - o   Finish the chapter. Start after the Reaction Awareness Exercise.

I am grateful for:

Wisdom I've learned:

What I am surrendering to God:

What I can actually change:

Scripture verse I will focus on to help me trust God:

Action steps I will take to improve my relationship with myself and God:

Action steps I will take to improve my relationship with others:

Session 7:

The Things I Can

EXERCISE REVIEW:

- Share about your experience with the two gratitude exercises in *Ditch the Drama*. **What did you discover about God?**
- Share about your experience with the Finding Forgiveness Exercise in *Ditch the Drama*. **Were you able to see from a new perspective?**

SESSION NOTES:

Once you understand how the trap of the drama triangle works, then you can take steps to prevent falling in. The most important tool in your toolbox will be your relationship with God.

When the world presses in and tries to tell you who you are, immediately turn to God. Let Him remind you of your value and identity. Let Him fill you with love. Then, respond to others out of that love.

Easier said than done, right? None of us are going to respond perfectly like Christ every time. But we can practice fighting our instincts and eventually respond out of love faster and more frequently.

Boundary Response

Healthy boundaries create a healthy balance between yourself and others. Tip the scales in either direction and you'll be left vulnerable. Too many boundaries will isolate you. Too few boundaries will leave you vulnerable.

Imbalance in either direction comes from the inability to trust God and leads to death. For one person it could be a death in relationships. For someone struggling with depression or suicide, it could mean literal death.

I don't mean to scare anyone. I only want us all to understand the importance of boundaries. They can be uncomfortable at first and easy to ignore or brush off. But they can also be the key to finding joy and freedom beyond what you ever expected.

There's no way to understand how immensely balanced boundaries will benefit you until you've put them into practice. So, take my word for it. They will rock your world! Keep your eyes on Jesus and step forward in courageous faith.

Creating healthy boundaries is a practice. There's no perfect way to do it. And it will probably be a little messy with trial and error. That's okay. Just don't delay in starting. You will never feel ready to create them.

Eventually, you will see your perspective begin to shift. Healthy boundaries will become easier to make. And then one day you'll be surprised when someone attempts to trample on your healthy boundaries. You'll wonder how you ever lived without them.

Before you start, ask God which boundaries to make and take down, when, where, and with whom. Make sure you have a healthy support system around you to keep you accountable and cheer you on!

When Leaving Isn't an Option: Building Internal Boundaries

When we identify an unhealthy person in our life, many of us will be able to remove them. We can cut off contact, change jobs, or get a divorce. But, in some cases, the option to cut off the relationship is impossible. It might be a family member or someone you share child custody with. It may be a spouse that God has asked you to continue walking with. So, how do you cope when you are forced to stay in relationship? Internal boundaries.

Because you cannot change the other person, staying in relationship with unhealthy people is extremely difficult. It takes tremendous patience and reliance on God to stay healthy and balanced. If you are struggling due to the relationship, that is completely normal. Give yourself grace; this is advanced boundary work.

> *"Behold, I send you out as sheep in the midst of wolves. Therefore be wise as serpents and harmless as doves."*
>
> Matthew 10:16 (NKJV)

Internal boundaries require that you are heavily rooted in your identity in Christ. So much so, that you will not react when your identity is challenged by accusations, lies,

or manipulation. Keep in mind, this person's behavior is their own responsibility and is not a reflection of your value.

First, examine the behavior the unhealthy person has shown. Are they often stuck in victim mentality? Do they have narcissistic tendencies? Does their behavior change quickly? Do they have an inflated view of their importance?

The more you understand about their patterns of behavior and thinking, the more prepared you will be for their reactions. You won't take them personally.

This is how Jesus was able to remain calm in the face of the Pharisees' accusations. He knew His identity was unshakable as the son of God. He knew the Pharisees were behaving out of their own brokenness. He shrewdly discerned what was going on beneath the surface while remaining harmless as a dove.

Start building a personal support system. Ask people who have successfully healed from unhealthy relationships to mentor you. Recruit trusted friends to keep you accountable. They can be a safe way to vent and process your emotions.

Then, make as many external boundaries as you can. Some examples include:

- Communicate the topics you will or will not discuss
- Communicate the times you will or will not be available
- Communicate the consequences if they ignore your boundaries

When they encroach on your boundaries (and they will because this is exactly what makes them unhealthy), be prepared with a plan. This way you can have a considered response instead of reacting. You may choose not to answer their call. When you are calm, you can text them. You may choose to say, "I love you, but I'm not having that conversation," followed by walking away. You may say "I am not prepared to respond, and I need more time to think about what you are saying."

Many unhealthy individuals are creating drama out of their own insecurities and impulses. Some, however, can be intentionally trying to hurt you. Even if you do not know their intentions or plans, God does. You serve a great big God who knows how to lead you. He can tell you exactly which steps to take and which words to use. And He can tell you when to be silent and when to pause.

While your journey may include more challenges than others, you can still experience joy and freedom. Just keep taking it S.L.O.W. one moment at a time:

- Surrender
- Listen
- Obey
- Worship

This does not have to be a heavy burden. Instead, see it as an opportunity to experience a closer relationship with God. Your trust in Him will build as He shows you how He can protect you. Your peace will increase when you keep your eyes on Him and not on your challenges.

The Serenity Prayer includes "accepting hardship as a pathway to peace" because God knows how to transform our struggles into victories.

The peace muscles will grow, but rarely will they develop overnight. In the meantime, use the tools and strategies below to stay healthy and balanced.

Survival Checklist:
- Stay rooted in your identity in Christ
- Feel your feelings in a safe space
- Process your feelings with trusted outsiders
- Recruit mentors
- Recruit several accountability partners
- Join a support group (Celebrate Recovery, CoDA, ACOA, Al Anon, etc.)
- Create a self-care plan, including time away
- Build external boundaries
- Read your Bible regularly
- Spend extended time in prayer and meditation
- Surrender to God moment by moment
- Follow God's will as best you can
- Regularly assess whether you have fallen into victim, rescuer, or aggressor perspectives
- Forgive, bless, and do good for the unhealthy person(s)
- Give yourself grace for your mistakes and reactions

DISCUSSION QUESTIONS:

1. Do you naturally find it easier to show love toward others or toward yourself?

2. What kind of boundaries are you employing in your relationships?

3. Are your current boundaries working to keep your relationships balanced?

4. Have you had any success with internal boundaries?

PRAYER:

Heavenly Father,
I reject any influences the world has had on my identity in the past. Help me to create healthy relationships and love others and myself through the process. I am truly grateful for all the blessings you have provided. I am humbled by your generosity even though I am still a sinner. I recognize that the anger and bitterness I've held on to have played a role in those sins. Please forgive me. Right now, I choose to forgive those who have hurt me as well. Bless them and help them to understand your love and grace. Bring peace to their mind and emotions. Heal any physical and emotional wounds they are suffering. In Jesus name, Amen.

HOMEWORK QUESTIONS:

1. Think about the different kinds of relationships in your life. How could your life improve by creating healthy boundaries?

2. In what areas could your life improve by removing unhealthy boundaries?

3. Against whom are you holding anger or resentments? Do you need to forgive people, God, or yourself?

4. Which resentment myths have you been using as an excuse to hold on to resent-ments?

5. This week, how can you love or bless those you are trying to forgive?

READING FOR NEXT SESSION IN *DITCH THE DRAMA*:
- Chapter 8 (Wisdom)
- Chapter 9 (To Know the Difference)
- Chapter 10 (Amen)

I am grateful for:

Wisdom I've learned:

What I am surrendering to God:

What I can actually change:

Scripture verse I will focus on to help me trust God:

Action steps I will take to improve my relationship with myself and God:

Action steps I will take to improve my relationship with others:

Session 8:

Wisdom to Know the Difference

SESSION NOTES:

Wisdom

Having all the facts in the world will not necessarily translate into wisdom. Most of us carry phones with access to every conceivable fact through the internet. Yet, so far, it seems like wisdom is on the decline.

Actually, wisdom is the practice of staying objective and consistently applying whatever knowledge is at your disposal. It's not a skill we automatically acquire, but it is a skill we can learn and improve upon over time.

Wisdom has three steps:
1) Stay objective.
2) Identify what you can and cannot change.
3) Change what you can while staying within God's will.

Staying Objective.

With all our previous discussion of emotions and reactions, we know that no one can stay objective 100% of the time. We need to allow time for grief and processing emotions to reach objectivity.

As we get better at recognizing our emotions, we also get better at navigating them. Eventually, we gain the ability to stay objective while identifying our emotions as they happen. Yes, we'll still need to feel and process those emotions later. But, as long as we are practicing the Serenity Prayer principles, we'll start seeing the situation objectively in real time.

Identifying What You Can and Cannot Change.

This step leaves a lot of room for interpretation. And that's on purpose. All of our circumstances and perspectives are different. God's plan for each of us in unique. Therefore, no perfect formula will fit everyone.

The knowledge you currently possess determines what you believe you have control over. As you gain more knowledge, your opinions of what you can and cannot change will grow. That is why the process of applying these steps is called a practice. It is not a static formula. It changes as your ideas transform.

At some point you will try to change the things you cannot change. When that happens, resist the urge to shame and berate yourself. Life is journey about growth and learning, not about being perfect. Beating yourself up will only keep you stuck.

Keep seeking God and His will. He will show you exactly what He wants you to see in each situation. This practice is not for the sake of being perfect, but for the sake of growing closer to God.

Changing What You Can While Staying Within God's Will.
The third step in wisdom is to walk in surrendered obedience to stay in God's will. That walk will look different in each season. Today it could look like an enormous leap of faith. And tomorrow it could be a quiet rest. Every step in every season is equally important.

The effectiveness of these wisdom steps and Serenity Prayer principles will improve as you consistently practice. Remember, what you are learning throughout this study is a healthy, Biblical lifestyle. This is not a fad. These tools are not band-aids that you'll be able to throw away once you see enough healing.

These practices come from God's word. They are His instructions. Embrace them and ditch the drama.

To Know the Difference
Perhaps even more difficult than coming to terms with our own emotions, is coming to terms with the emotions of others. Each of us has different instincts and wounds and ways of seeing the world. Honestly, I think it's a miracle any of us ever learn to work together for more than a few days. (But God!)

Creating lasting, healthy relationships takes time. Get curious about other people, especially when you don't completely agree with them. That curiosity will not necessarily lead us to understand or agree with one another. Stay determined to accept the other

person where they are at and respect them. That way, love and trust have an opportunity to take root.

God does not smite everyone who does not agree with Him. He accepts us and loves us into a relationship that transforms our lives. Jesus did the same and asks us to follow suit.

Now, this does not mean we are to blindly accept all people into our lives in all seasons. We get to use our boundaries and decide who stays for a season or a lifetime. But, in order to make wise decisions, we also need to observe those around us.

Yes, we can trust God to bring the right people into our lives. Unfortunately, not all of them will be the right people to support us. Some will be the right people to teach us an important lesson. How can we know which is which? By observing whether their words and actions line up.

As a young adult I was sure liars and manipulators would be easy to spot. I just followed my heart. If someone made me feel accepted and loved, then I stopped questioning their motives and behavior. Like most humans, I assumed everyone lived by my same upstanding morals and motives. I was very wrong.

I learned the hard way that actions are much more important to understanding a person than their words. Words are easy to say and, for some, they are tools to deceive. But actions speak louder than words.

Guidelines to building healthy relationships:

- **Trust takes time to build.** If someone you barely know is expecting or demanding your full trust, that is a red flag. If you are the one expecting others to trust you within a few meetings, then it's time to lower your expectations. Healthy trust is built over time.
- **You're drawn to what's comfortable.** If your family valued military service, then you will likely be drawn to those who value the same. If you grew up in a family with addicts and codependents, then you'll likely be drawn to addicts and codependents. So, if you want something different from your relationships, then choose a healthy uncomfortable.

- **First impressions are not always accurate.** If someone wants your trust, then they are likely to be on their best behavior. At best, this is sucking up. At worst, this is manipulative love-bombing. Stay vigilant and continue to observe.
- **Recognize whether they own their mistakes.** There are individuals who will accuse anyone or anything else rather than admit their own flaws. Do not be swayed by their excuses. Even if they are acting from a place of insecurity, they will create more drama.
- **Respect boundaries.** Don't force anyone to move faster in a relationship than they are comfortable. And don't let anyone force you beyond what is comfortable for you. Balanced relationships include respect on both sides of the street.
- **No one is perfect.** Expect to have disagreements in relationships. The key is to be honest and work toward helping each other grow.
- **Everyone is equal.** If you see yourself as above or below the other person, it's time to look inward and surrender to God's truth.
- **Everyone changes.** As time passes, we all change. Life has a way of changing our beliefs and behaviors. Allow people space to grow and change. Ultimately, two people seeking God will grow together in Him.

Amen

Amen is only the beginning. God is leading you toward living a life to the full. You get to decide daily whether you choose to follow.

> *"Jesus said, "If you hold to my teaching, you are really my disciples. Then you will know the truth, and the truth will set you free.""*

John 8:32

Your chance at freedom is available, but it requires practicing the principles in the Serenity Prayer.

In my healing journey, I had every excuse in the book to follow my own path. I wanted a vacation. I was bored. I wanted an easier way. I didn't believe it was necessary to keep it up once I got "better."

But every time I went my own way, drama came back with a vengeance. It was harder and harder to get back on God's path. There's more risk in complacency than we realize.

Walking away from these practices will bring you right back to a drama-riddled lifestyle and the cycle continues.

DISCUSSION QUESTIONS:

1. What prevents you from getting curious about others?

2. What prevents you from staying objective?

3. Has it been easy or difficult to discern the things you can and cannot change? Why?

4. Review the guidelines to building healthy relationships. Which guidelines do you forget most often?

PRAYER:

Heavenly Father,
I leave all of my relationships and loved ones in your hands. Help me to see them as you see them. I ask for your wisdom in navigating relationships so that I may become more like Jesus. Thank you for the strength and willingness to continue practicing the Serenity Prayer. I know that your plan is better than anything I could imagine. Give me eyes to see your hand in my life so that I will be consistently drawn back to your loving arms.
In Jesus' name, Amen.

HOMEWORK QUESTIONS:

1. Now that you have all the tools, examine one area of your life that has been difficult to deal with recently and apply the Serenity Prayer.

a) What are you powerless to change in this situation?

b) How can you change your response or perspective?

c) What is God asking you to do next?

2. Who in your life previously, or right now, did you have a difficult confrontation with, or tried repeatedly NOT to have a confrontation with? How could you have made it an opportunity for discovery rather than confrontation or avoidance?

3. Which wisdom principle could you apply to a current situation or relationship?

4. We will always need to apply these Biblical principles to our life in every season. This is a lifestyle, not just a course. What kind of support system can you begin to build that will help you continue cultivating these new, healthy habits?

I am grateful for:

Wisdom I've learned:

What I am surrendering to God:

What I can actually change:

Scripture verse I will focus on to help me trust God:

Action steps I will take to improve my relationship with myself and God:

Action steps I will take to improve my relationship with others:

Bonus Session:

Codependency and Narcissism

SESSION NOTES:

Codependency and Narcissism

I doubt there's ever been an unhealthy pairing more common in human history than codependents and narcissists. These two have unhealthy tendencies that, at first, appear to suit each other perfectly but, over time, are revealed to be destructive.

It's commonly thought that codependents and narcissists attract because they are exact opposites. However, below the surface, these two have a lot more in common than you'd expect. It's the commonalities that help codependents and narcissists understand one another. It's their differences that feed their dysfunction.

Neither one is better than the other. They are both children of God struggling to make sense of their value and place in the world.

Core Identity

Codependents lack a solid, independent identity. At their core, they rely on others' opinions to define their sense of self and value.
Narcissists also lack a solid, independent identity. At their core, they rely on others' opinions to define their sense of self and value.

Motivation

Both personality types are motivated by concealing their insecurities, fear, and shame from others. Don't take this personally though. They are trying to hide the truth from themselves first and foremost.

Codependents and narcissists are terrified that they are worthless. They both use complex coping strategies to prove themselves valuable. The strategies help each one stay in denial of their true weaknesses. Unfortunately, these elaborate strategies only get in the way of true surrender.

Goals

The strategies codependents and narcissists use to maintain their sense of validation always include other people. But how they use people is very different.

Codependents believe they are only as valuable as others' need for them. That's why they concentrate on meeting others' needs at the expense of their own. They think, "I must be important because I help needy people. Without a needy person, I am worthless."

This is why so many codependents find it hard to leave hurting addicts. Their value is found in helping. They see walking away from a hurting person as proof they have no value. In reality, walking away would establish a healthy boundary.

But codependents do not need an addict to feel valuable. They will use any needy person to fill their desire for value.

Narcissists believe they are only as valuable as they are important. And proof of their importance comes from others meeting their needs. The more others meet a narcissist's needs, the more secure they are in their fantasy.

They think "I must be important because you are meeting my needs. If you stop, then there is something wrong with you." And they will not have a problem telling you just how "wrong" you are.

Narcissists concentrate on meeting their own needs at the expense of others. They may appear compassionate, but only if it serves their ultimate goal of having their needs met.

Warped Narrative

Codependents live in a world of compassion. They cannot imagine living any other way. The idea of using others to meet their personal needs is completely outside their comprehension.

In relationships with a narcissist, codependents focus on everything they have in common. The underlying shame and need to hide their insecurities feel familiar. Empathy abounds. Codependents assume they both have the same motivations to serve others. As a result, codependents take the words of the narcissist at face value.

As the true colors of the narcissist are revealed, codependents will downplay the red flags. They cling to their false sense of value by making excuses for the narcissist's behavior. "They aren't really that bad. What they said is true, even if it was hurtful."

Narcissists live in a world of their own importance. They cannot imagine living any other way. The idea of meeting others' needs before their own is a terrifying prospect.

In relationships with codependents, narcissists love-bomb and flatter. They say they agree with your opinions. They promise what they never intend to give. They give gifts in order to appear like they've sacrificed. They will blame their mistakes on you or someone else. They will claim to be the victim rather than admit fault. All this to stay in their fantasy of importance.

They will *not* go out of their way to sacrifice for someone else. Their words will *not* line up with their actions. Rather than admit to themselves they are equal to others, they go in search of another codependent to prove their importance.

Appearance
How they appear on the outside is a different matter. Codependents desire to be what others need. They have a habit of becoming chameleons and adjusting to fit their audience. A confident on-the-job problem solver becomes a needy victim when calling their best friend.

Narcissists appear like a knight in shining armor. They will directly tell you about their accomplishments and what they've done for others. In relationships, narcissists will explain why they are not only important, but also necessary. This leaves others feeling guilty or stupid for wanting to cut ties.

Again, both approaches are designed to keep relationships to validate their sense of self and value. They are two sides of the same coin.

Review the illustration to see how they are connected on a continuum. Keep in mind, codependents can embody some narcissistic traits. They do this out of desperation to keep their sense of self and value. Narcissists will display the overly-empathetic traits of a codependent to get what they want for a short time. This is not a sign of true change.

Codependent and Narcissistic Patterns

Narcissistic

- Needs to feel important
- Puts their own needs ahead of others' needs
- Fearful of losing relationships
  (specifically being important)
- Trying to feel important enough
- Overcompensates for their insecurities, fears,
  and/or shame through power/influence
- Rarely empathizes
- Often manipulates or accuses to get what they want

- Lacks a solid, independent identity
- Relies on others' opinions to define a sense of self and value
- Can attempt to control others to preserve sense of self
- Tells themselves how others "must feel" in order to preserve their value
- Obsesses about how others see them rather than seeing others

Codependent

- Needs to be needed or appreciated
- Puts others' needs ahead of their own
- Fearful of losing relationships
  (specifically being needed)
- Trying to feel good enough
- Overcompensates for their insecurities, fears,
  and/or shame by helping
- Over-empathizes
- Often burns out to give others what they want

Healing from
Codependent and Narcissistic Patterns

Codependent

- Identify and meet their own needs
- Start identifying their opinions and goals
- Start saying "no."
- Stop taking responsibility others' feelings

- Focus on building an identity in Christ
- Allow others to make their own decisions according to their own personal desires
- See yourself as equal to others
- See others' needs as equal to your own
- Share insecurities, fear, and shame with trusted, healthy individuals
- Nurture relationships with healthy balance and boundaries
- Identify motivations for interpersonal interactions
- Act without alterior motives or expecting anything in return

Narcissistic

- Choose integrity over their own needs
- Become honest and forthcoming
- Treat others with respect
- Take responsibility for self-centeredness

Destructive Cycles

When either a codependent or narcissist has reached their tolerance limit, they will explode. A narcissist will explode because their needs aren't being met well enough. A codependent will explode because they're not being appreciated.

The offending party will apologize and promise to change. Due to the underlying need to keep their sense of value through the other person, the apology is usually accepted. Unfortunately, the cycle will only continue and become more destructive until one or both parties leaves or changes.

Healing from Codependency and Narcissism

Codependents are more likely to seek healing than narcissists. However, with God and personal determination, anyone can heal from either set of patterns. We don't have to stay stuck. But we do have to choose change for ourselves.

The most foundational piece of healing comes from gaining a solid identity in Christ. We are all searching for our sense of self and value. And we are made whole when we let God define our identity.

Once codependents recognize this at their core, they will stop needing others' approval. They can finally focus on what they need for themselves and meet those needs. Suddenly, their motives change. They can help others out of a pure desire to help.

They will not need anything in return. Giving is an act of love rather than an obligation.

When narcissists accept their identity in Christ, they will start accepting the importance of others' needs. They can finally rest in knowing their importance in God's plan is enough. Helping meet others' needs can be done out of a desire to show God's love. They will not need anything in return. Giving becomes an act of humility rather than manipulation.

Embracing this healing process helps both sides gain clarity. How they view each other changes as their minds are renewed. Recovering codependents are repelled by the red flags of narcissistic behavior. Recovering narcissists will be repelled by the unhealthy needs of the codependent. Healthy people are attracted to healthy people.

Once again, we see the problems we experience can be healed from the inside out rather than trying to change others from the outside in.

NPD and Gaslighting

Narcissistic Personality Disorder (NPD) takes narcissism to the next level. This is where hurting others is the goal. Although they may appear charming and empathetic, an NPD person's need for power and complete lack of empathy make them particularly devious.

Those with NPD will seek to secure a codependent partner by love-bombing with grandiose gestures. Part of the love-bombing process includes lots of questions about the codependent. The codependent feels seen and valued, but the NPD person has an ulterior motive. They are looking to build a profile of the codependent so they can pretend to be what the codependent desires.

Once the individual with NPD feels they have gained the trust and commitment of the codependent, their behavior changes to reveal their true motives. Unfortunately, if the codependent trusts the predator, they may downplay and ignore the red flags. This, of course, is what the NPD person is hoping for.

Gaslighting is a technique heavily used by those with NPD. The goal is to confuse the victim into distrusting their feelings and eventually their reality. Gaslighting incorporates a copious amount of lies and deflections. The NPD person will even go so far as to minimize feelings, dismiss opinions, and question memories. As a result, the codependent relies entirely upon their NPD partner to interpret their reality.

There is a great deal of literature explaining NPD and gaslighting. While those with NPD are a small percentage of the population, they are prolific in the number of people they harm. They have the ability to pursue power while still appearing genuine and friendly with most people.

If you feel you are in a relationship with someone with NPD, seek professional help immediately. Do not attempt to confront the NPD person head on. That will only alert them to change their tactics. There are strategies that will help you leave safely. Create a plan and a support system before taking action.

DISCUSSION QUESTIONS:

1. Which patterns within codependency, narcissism, and Narcissistic Personality Disorder stood out to you most? Why?

2. Has this lesson on codependency and narcissism changed the way you see yourself or those around you? How?

3. What steps could you take this week to bolster your identity in Christ?

PRAYER:

Heavenly Father,
Thank you for sealing my identity in Christ. I know that your declaration of my value is the only definitive proof I need. But sometimes I forget and I fall into old patterns. Remove my unbelief, Father. Help me incorporate my true value into every inch of my spirit, soul, and body. I release the codependents and narcissists in my life to you. I trust you to hold them and guide them. Help me to build healthy boundaries with them rather than attempt to change them.
In Jesus' name, Amen.

HOMEWORK QUESTIONS:

1. Have you ever attempted to change a person with codependent or narcissistic tendencies? What were the results?

2. What would it look like to keep healthy boundaries with a codependent?

3. What would it look like to keep healthy boundaries with a narcissist?

4. Have you adopted any patterns of codependency or narcissism?

5. Which healing patterns will you adopt instead?

6. If you are currently in a relationship with someone who displays the patterns of Narcissistic Personality Disorder, what steps will you take this week to seek professional help? Build a support system?

I am grateful for:

Wisdom I've learned:

What I am surrendering to God:

What I can actually change:

Scripture verse I will focus on to help me trust God:

Action steps I will take to improve my relationship with myself and God:

Action steps I will take to improve my relationship with others:

Notes for Facilitators

Welcome, Facilitator! Praise God for your courage to say "yes" and facilitate this study! You're a hero helping to make joy and freedom available to others just by showing up.

Don't worry, you don't have to meet any special requirements to get this group going. Just have a willingness to trust God, follow the instructions for each week, and participate in the study yourself. It's God's responsibility to show up and touch each member's heart.

BEFORE THE STUDY BEGINS:
- Encourage each participant to purchase both the *Ditch the Drama* book (or e-book) and *Ditch the Drama Study Guide* before the first session.
- Decide when and where the group will meet and communicate that to the group. This does not have to be in person – groups have met virtually with participants based all over the country using online meeting software!
- Make sure you'll have internet access to stream the videos and watch as a group.
- Decide whether the group will read the session notes before watching the video or read them together after the video. There's no right or wrong way to do this, it's whatever you feel most comfortable with. Whatever you decide, share that information with the group so they know how to prepare for each session.
- The session notes below are just recommendations for each session. Feel free to adjust the format according to what works for your group.

Session 1 Notes:
- Welcome everyone to the group!
- Start with introductions and have each person share a couple interesting facts about themselves as an icebreaker.
- Watch the Session 1 Video.
- Read the session notes out loud (if they have not already done so at home).
- Review these Initial Group Guidelines with the members and then ask if they'd like to add any specific guidelines that would help everyone feel they are in a safe environment. Initial Group Guidelines:
    - This group is a judgment-free, comparison-free, mask-free, shame-free group!
    - Everyone's responses and opinions are welcome, valued, and respected.
- Review the Discussion Questions as a group. Give everyone a chance to respond. Don't be afraid of awkward silences. Some people are not comfortable speaking up and need more time to formulate a response or build courage to speak up. Let everyone know their opinions are valued and respected.
- Ask if there is anything else anyone would like to add about what they are discovering so far through this study.
- Take prayer requests and read the session's prayer out loud to close.

Session 2 Notes:
- Welcome everyone to the group!
- Watch the Session 2 Video.
- Read the session notes out loud (if they have not already done so at home).
- Review the Discussion Questions as a group. Give everyone a chance to respond. Don't be afraid of awkward silences. Some people are not comfortable speaking up and need more time to formulate a response or build courage to speak up. Let everyone know their opinions are valued and respected.
- Ask if there is anything else anyone would like to add about what they are discovering so far through this study.
- Read the session's prayer out loud to close.

Session 3 Notes:
- Welcome everyone to the group!
- Review the exercise from the reading homework in *Ditch the Drama*.
- Watch the Session 3 Video.
- Read the session notes out loud (if they have not already done so at home).
- Review the Discussion Questions as a group. Give everyone a chance to respond. Don't be afraid of awkward silences. Some people are not comfortable speaking up and need more time to formulate a response or build courage to speak up. Let everyone know their opinions are valued and respected.
- Ask if there is anything else anyone would like to add about what they are discovering so far through this study.
- Read the session's prayer out loud to close.

Session 4 Notes:
- Welcome everyone to the group!
- Review the exercises from the reading homework in *Ditch the Drama*.
- Watch the Session 4 Video.
- Read the session notes out loud (if they have not already done so at home).
- Review the Discussion Questions as a group. Give everyone a chance to respond. Don't be afraid of awkward silences. Some people are not comfortable speaking up and need more time to formulate a response or build courage to speak up. Let everyone know their opinions are valued and respected.
- Ask if there is anything else anyone would like to add about what they are discovering so far through this study.
- Read the session's prayer out loud to close.

Session 5 Notes:
- Welcome everyone to the group!
- Review the exercise from the reading homework in *Ditch the Drama*.
- Watch the Session 5 Video.
- Read the session notes out loud (if they have not already done so at home).
- Review the Discussion Questions as a group. Give everyone a chance to respond. Don't be afraid of awkward silences. Some people are not comfortable speaking up and need more time to formulate a response or build courage to speak up. Let everyone know their opinions are valued and respected.

- Ask if there is anything else anyone would like to add about what they are discovering so far through this study.
- Read the session's prayer out loud to close.

Session 6 Notes:

- Welcome everyone to the group!
- Review the exercises from the reading homework in *Ditch the Drama*.
- Watch the Session 6 Video.
- Read the session notes out loud (if they have not already done so at home).
- Review the Discussion Questions as a group. Give everyone a chance to respond. Don't be afraid of awkward silences. Some people are not comfortable speaking up and need more time to formulate a response or build courage to speak up. Let everyone know their opinions are valued and respected.
- Ask if there is anything else anyone would like to add about what they are discovering so far through this study.
- Read the session's prayer out loud to close.

Session 7 Notes:

- Welcome everyone to the group!
- Review the exercises from the reading homework in *Ditch the Drama*.
- Watch the Session 7 Video.
- Read the session notes out loud (if they have not already done so at home).
- Review the Discussion Questions as a group. Give everyone a chance to respond. Don't be afraid of awkward silences. Some people are not comfortable speaking up and need more time to formulate a response or build courage to speak up. Let everyone know their opinions are valued and respected.
- Ask if there is anything else anyone would like to add about what they are discovering so far through this study.
- Read the session's prayer out loud to close.

Session 8 Notes:
- Welcome everyone to the group!
- Watch the Session 8 Video.
- Read the session notes out loud (if they have not already done so at home).
- Review the Discussion Questions as a group. Give everyone a chance to respond. Don't be afraid of awkward silences. Some people are not comfortable speaking up and need more time to formulate a response or build courage to speak up. Let everyone know their opinions are valued and respected.
- Ask if there is anything else anyone would like to add about what they are discovering so far through this study.
- Read the session's prayer out loud to close.

BONUS Session 9 Notes (optional):
- Welcome everyone to the group!
- There is no video for this session.
- Read the session notes out loud (if they have not already done so at home).
- Review the Discussion Questions as a group. Give everyone a chance to respond. Don't be afraid of awkward silences. Some people are not comfortable speaking up and need more time to formulate a response or build courage to speak up. Let everyone know their opinions are valued and respected.
- Ask if there is anything else anyone would like to add about what they are discovering so far through this study.
- Read the session's prayer out loud to close.

Session 10 Notes (optional):
- In this last session, share a meal together to celebrate and discuss all that you have learned and accomplished so far! Looking back on how far we've come encourages us and gives us hope to keep growing one baby step at a time!
- Go around the group and have each person share one thing they have accepted they cannot change, one thing they have changed, and one nugget of wisdom they'll take with them moving forward.

About the Author

Born with her right arm stopping just below the elbow, Ginny is known as the Single Handed Serenity Coach specializing in trauma recovery. Her recovery journey from codependency, alcoholism, and panic attacks taught her to trust God with the deep, broken parts of her heart. Ginny inspires audiences worldwide by embracing her physical difference with humor and joy as the co-host of the Telly Award winning Bloom Today TV show, found on 17 broadcast TV networks in over 200 countries and on Amazon Prime. She also co-hosts The Christian View and Recovery Strategies 4Life TV shows.

Ginny is also the author of *Ditch the Drama* and several workbooks, including *Bloom Forward* and *Bloom Today Workbook*. Her numerous online courses, including "Recovery Strategies 4Life," "The Trust Challenge," "You are Priceless Bootcamp," and "Trust Academy" are hosted on bloom-u.org. Ginny also serves as Vice President of Bloom In The Dark, Inc., a global charity raising awareness for men and women coming out of brokenness and abuse that they are not alone and there is hope.

For Further Healing

A journal to renew your mind...
one day at a time.

Use this 90 day devotional journal with assessments and daily questions will help you build new thought patterns, muscle memories, and neural pathways.

Videos & Coaching Tools
by
Ginny Priz & Paula Mosher Wallace
Based on the Bloom Today TV show

BloomTodayTV.com

Life is messy, but you don't have to be drawn into all the soul-sucking drama!

Learn how as Ginny Priz unpacks the Serenity Prayer in her book

Ditch The Drama

Learn more at
ditchthedrama.net

Look inside

A collection of Christian courses designed to bring hope and healing to anyone coming out of pain, abuse, or addictions.

bloom-u.org

Do you struggle with

- ☑ PTSD - Complex Trauma
- ☑ Any type of Abuse
- ☑ Addictions
- ☑ Loss
- ☑ Depression
- ☑ Fear - Stress - Anxiety
- ☑ Codependency
- ☑ Plateaued recovery